THE Dandy ANNUAL 2025

THIS BOOK BELONGS TO

_ _ _ _ _ _ _ _ _ _ _ _ _ _

DIRECTOR OF MISCHIEF
Mike Stirling

DIRECTOR OF MAYHEM
Craig Graham

EDITORIAL DIRECTOR (KIDS)
Gareth Whelan

EDITOR
John Anderson

CONTENT EDITOR
Claire Bartlett

PRODUCTION MANAGER
Michelle O'Donnell

SUB EDITOR
Leah Barton

SENIOR DESIGNER
Dawn Cochlan

DESIGNER
Mark McIlmail

CONTRIBUTORS
Nigel Auchterlounie
Nigel Parkinson
Wayne Thompson
Ned Hartley
Andy Fanton

Iain McLaughlin
Lew Stringer
Nick Brennan
Steve Bright
Gary Boller

Mychailo Kazybrid
Faz Choudhury
Steve Beckett
Barrie Appleby
Kate Ashwin

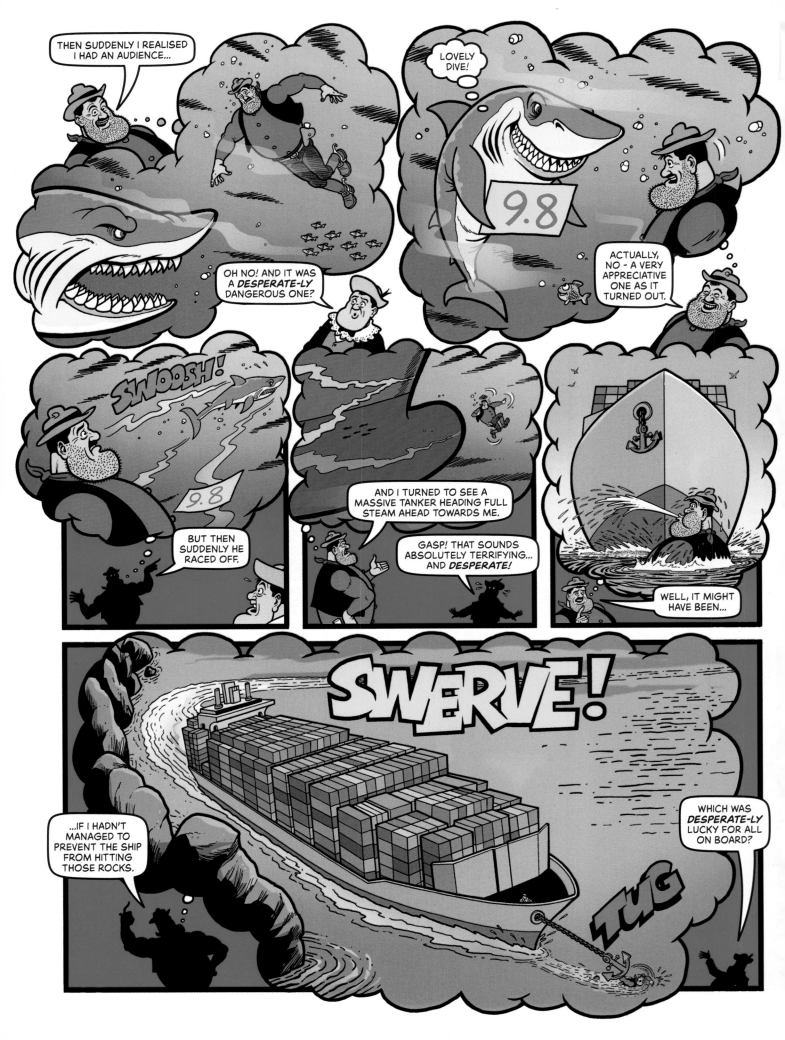

BERYL THE PERIL

George   Harry   Noah   Olivia   Emily   Meera

DANDYTOWN SCOUTS!   NEVER PREPARED!

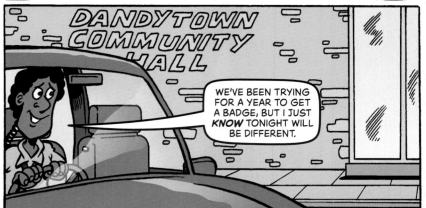

WE'VE BEEN TRYING FOR A YEAR TO GET A BADGE, BUT I JUST *KNOW* TONIGHT WILL BE DIFFERENT.

SEE? MY SCOUTS ARE SO KEEN THEY'RE HERE ALREADY. HI, KIDS!

KIDS? KIDS? HELLO?!

YUP, THERE THEY ARE, ALL EAGER AND KEEN. SIGH...

WHAT ARE YOU ALL LOOKING AT?

A CUTE CAT!

IT'S A PURR FACTORY.

OKAY, LET THE CAT GO HOME AND WE CAN GO INSIDE TO THINK ABOUT MAYBE GETTING A BADGE.

I THINK I'M HAVING AN IDEA... AND IT'S A WINNER! IT'S...

...A PET-CARE BADGE!

YOU'RE RIGHT, THERE IS A BADGE FOR THAT.

I KNOW WHICH PET I CAN LOOK AFTER, BACK IN A BIT.

ANY OTHER IDEAS ABOUT WHAT WE COULD DO FOR A BADGE?

THERE'S A BADGE JUST ABOUT CARING FOR CATS.

CORPORAL CLOTT

CLOTT!

YOU RANG, M'LORD?

CLOTT, WHY IS THERE A PAINTING OF MY CAR ON THE PARADE GROUND?!

IT'S NOT A PAINTING, SIR!

IT'S MY ACTUAL CAR!

WHY IS IT FLATTER THAN A PANCAKE IN A TROUSER PRESS?!

IT'S POSSIBLE I MAY HAVE RUN OVER IT IN A TANK.

IT'S 2D! HOW MANY TIMES DID YOU RUN OVER IT?

ALL THE TIMES!

THAT'S IT! YOU'RE GOING TO WORK IN THE CANTEEN! MAYBE THERE YOU WON'T...

YOU TRIED ME IN THE CANTEEN, REMEMBER?

THAT'S RIGHT! I HAD TO SPEND TWO WEEKS ON THE TOILET AFTER I ATE THAT PIE YOU MADE.

THE LAUNDRY THEN.

YOU SENT ME THERE TOO, REMEMBER?

YES, I REMEMBER.

I'VE TRIED YOU IN THE GARAGE, THE GUARD TOWER, THE RADAR ROOM AND EVEN THE BAND!

TRUMP!!!

OF COURSE! INSTEAD OF ME TRYING TO FIGURE OUT WHERE YOU FIT, I'LL GET THE CAREERS OFFICE TO FIGURE IT OUT.

THE WHAT OFFICE?

SO...

HERE AT THE CAREERS OFFICE, WE TEST YOU TO SEE WHERE YOU FIT BEST IN THE ARMY.

A TEST?

YES, ARE YOU READY?

YES!

DID I GET IT RIGHT? AM I READY?

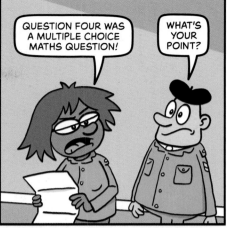

CUDDLES AND DIMPLES

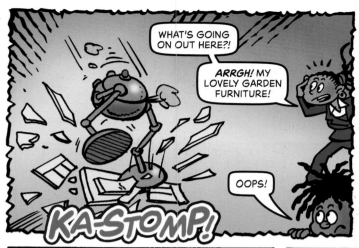

DREADLOCK HOLMES

DANDYCRAFT!

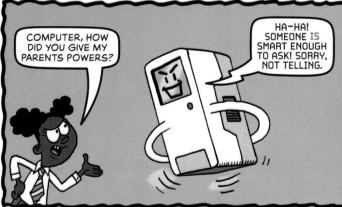

PART 1

LAYLA AND KANE ASK THE COMPUTER WHAT'S HAPPENED...

YOU SPEND SO MUCH TIME ON THAT GAME, I THOUGHT YOU WOULD ENJOY IT IF I CHANGED THE WORLD TO BE MORE LIKE IT.

I DO!

LAYLA AND KANE LEAVE TO TRY OUT THEIR NEW POWERS...

NOT ASKING ME HOW I CHANGED THE WHOLE WORLD?

OKAY!

HA-HA-HA! YOU WILL FLIP YOUR BISCUITS WHEN YOU FIND OUT! HA-HA-HA!

ALL ACROSS DANDYTOWN, THE SAME THING HAPPENS...

HUH?

I'M IN A LOG CABIN?

THE WORLD'S CHANGED!

HOW DID THIS HAPPEN?

PEOPLE OF DANDYTOWN!

HOW DO YOU LIKE YOUR NEW WORLD AND YOUR NEW RULERS?!

LOVE IT, THANKS! I'VE GOT A GAME JUST LIKE THIS!

I FORGOT TO MENTION WE'RE EVIL.

WAIT A DINAH MO! WE WON'T LET ANYONE EVIL LEAD US!

ZAP!

COUGH! WE WON'T LET ANYONE LEAD US WHO HASN'T GOT ZAPPY POWERS.

DANDYTOWN SCOUTS! NEVER PREPARED!

MMM... YES, OBVIOUSLY.

MEERA'S NOT HAPPY ABOUT SOMETHING.

WHATEVER.

SHE'S ON THE PHONE TO ONE OF THE OTHER SCOUT LEADERS.

YEAH, THAT IS A LOT OF BADGES.

LET ME JUST MUTE YOU FOR A SECOND.

TAP!

ARRGH! IT'S NOT FAIR!

DON'T WORRY, BABES, YOU'LL GET A BADGE SOON.

OKAY, GOTTA GO. BYE.

I CANNOT STAND HER!

WHY DOES SHE GET TO YOU SO BAD?

BECAUSE SHE'S ALWAYS SO SMUG ABOUT HAVING SO MANY BADGES!

DESPERATE DAN

CORPORAL CLOTT

THE ARMY HAS DECIDED THAT THE BEST PLACE FOR CORPORAL CLOTT IS NOT IN THE ARMY, SO THEY'RE HELPING HIM FIND A NEW JOB...

SO, WHAT DO YOU WANT TO BE NOW?

AN ASTRONAUT!

BE REALISTIC! YOU CAN'T BE AN ASTRONAUT.

DANDYTOWN DOESN'T EVEN HAVE A SPACE PROGRAMME.

DANDY SPACE CENTRE

VACANCIES

WHAT'S THAT THEN?

I GUESS WE'RE DOING THIS!

INSIDE...

HI, I'M AN ARMY CAREERS OFFICER LOOKING TO PLACE SOMEONE WHO'S RECENTLY LEFT THE ARMY.

IS IT THAT GUY TRYING TO FIGURE OUT HOW TO SIT IN A CHAIR?

DANDY SPACE CENTRE

YES.

FOLLOW ME FOR THE TESTS.

BUT...

ARRGH! GET ME AWAY FROM THIS PLACE!

HAVE YOU SEEN HOW SMALL THE DINNERS ARE?!

TESTING

RELAX!

SPACE DINNER

THERE'S NOT MUCH ROOM ON THE ROCKET, SO THE MEALS ARE DRIED, REMOVING THE WATER SHRINKS THEM.

WE JUST ADD WATER TO MAKE THEM BIG AGAIN.

YUM!

SQUIRT! GROW!

THIS IS A COPY OF THE CONTROLS IN A ROCKET. TRY PRESSING THE CORRECT BUTTON TO LAUNCH IT.

TESTING

OH, ER...

...THIS ONE?

NO, THAT WOULD HAVE DESTROYED THE ROCKET.

THIS ONE?

ALSO DESTROYED.

THIS?

THIS?

THIS?

THIS?

DESTROYED.

DESTROYED.

DESTROYED.

DESTROYED.

THE BUTTON TO LAUNCH HAS 'LAUNCH' WRITTEN ON IT!

DESTROY LAUNCH DESTROY

WHY ARE THESE OTHER BUTTONS EVEN HERE?!

MOVING ON!

THIS WILL TEST YOUR RESISTANCE TO G-FORCE BY SPINNING YOU AROUND. WE CAN SUBJECT YOU TO GRAVITY MANY TIMES STRONGER THAN OUR OWN.

NICE!

CUDDLES AND DIMPLES

BERYL THE PERIL

IT'S THE MIDDLE OF THE NIGHT AND A BLOODCURDLING SCREAM IS HEARD FROM FROM HYDE CASTLE...

ARRGH!

MASTER HYDE'S VAMPIRE BUTLER, MR SHRIEK, RUSHES TO THE RESCUE...

HOLD ON, MASTER HYDE!

SURVIVE A MOMENT LONGER!

WHAT IS IT?

DID THE UNNAMED THING IN THE BASEMENT ESCAPE AGAIN?

HAS THE INDESCRIBABLE HORROR IN THE ATTIC FOUND ITS WAY OUT?

DID THE TOILET BEAST GET YOU?

NO, I SURPRISED MYSELF WITH A PUMP.

I'M STARTING TO THINK YOU MIGHT NOT BE THE MONSTROUS VILLAIN YOUR GREAT-GRANDFATHER WAS!

A TEST IS CALLED FOR! HERE'S A PUPPY I HAPPENED TO HAVE HIDDEN AROUND MY PERSON!

FOR ME?!

SOON...

I SEE YOU'VE TUCKED HIM INTO BED AND UPLOADED 89 PHOTOS TO SOCIAL MEDIA.

WHAT WAS I MEANT TO DO?

EAT IT!

YOUR GREAT-GRANDFATHER WOULD OFTEN BERATE ME CRUELLY FOR HOURS.

TRY THAT!

WHAT DOES BERATE MEAN?

TO CRITICISE ANGRILY. I'LL PREPARE BY COWERING IN FEAR FIRST... OKAY, GO!

OOH, ER...

...YOU'RE A NAUGHTY NIGEL!

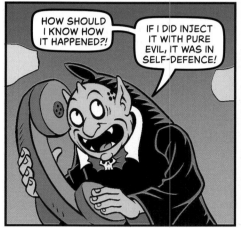

DESPERATE DAN

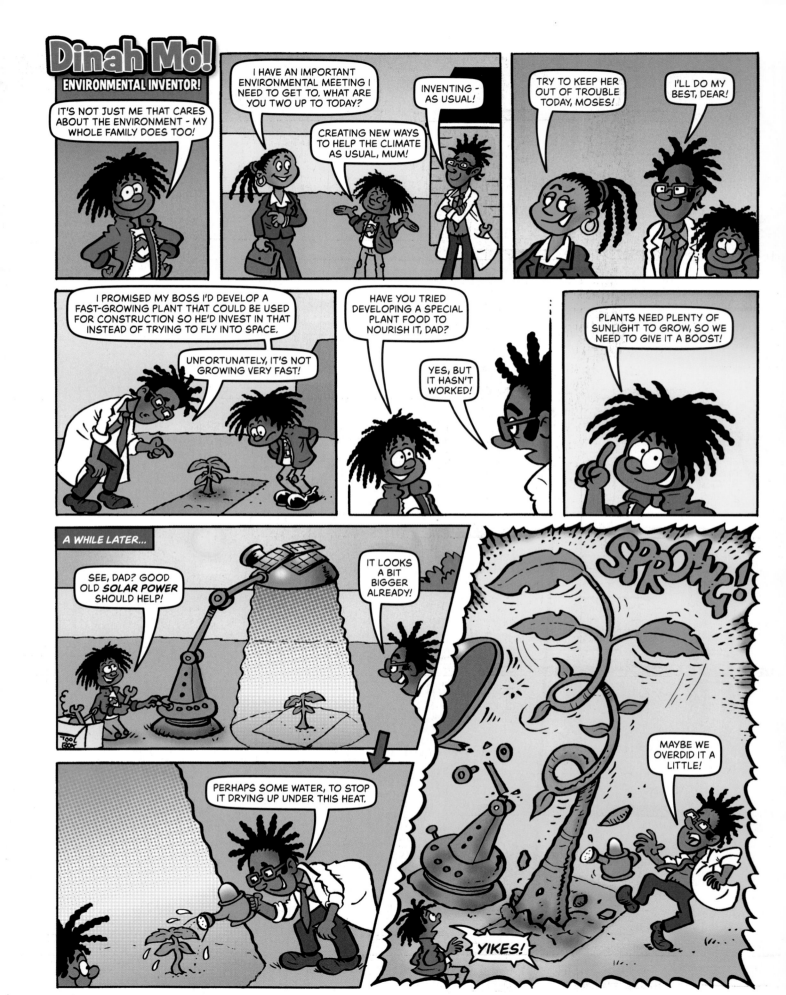

CORPORAL CLOTT

THE ARMY CAREERS OFFICER IS STILL TRYING TO FIND CORPORAL CLOTT A NEW JOB...

I COULD BE A BUILDER!

HMM... YOU WITH CRANES AND DIGGERS?

WHEEEE!

CRASH!

I THINK WE'LL TRY YOU IN AN OFFICE INSTEAD.

A WHAT?!

CLOTT'S CAREERS OFFICER GETS HIM A TRIAL PLACEMENT IN AN OFFICE...

WE'LL START YOU WITH SIMPLE DATA INPUT.

AWESOME, WHAT'S DATA?

DATA IS FACTS.

LOVE IT, AND WHAT'S INPUT AGAIN?

WHEN THE DATA IS PUT IN THE COMPUTER,

NICE... WHAT'S DATA AGAIN?

AN HOUR LATER...

LET'S START AGAIN, PRESS RETURN.

THIS?

DOINK!

THAT'S THE SPACE BAR.

ONE WRONG CLICK LATER...

NO! WHAT DID YOU DO?!

WHAT JUST HAPPENED?!

WHERE DID EVERYTHING GO?!

UH-OH

YOU'VE WIPED THE SERVER!

WHAT'S A SERVER?

IT'S THE MAIN COMPUTER ALL THE COMPUTERS ARE CONNECTED TO - AND NOW THERE'S NOTHING ON IT!

YOU'RE WELCOME!

IT WAS ALL BACKED UP. TAKE A BREAK WHILE I SORT IT, THE COFFEE'S OVER THERE.

COFFEE? THAT'S A DRINK, YEAH?

SHOVE!

CLOTT TRIES COFFEE...

SLURP!

SPLURT!!!

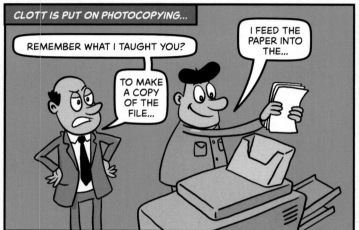

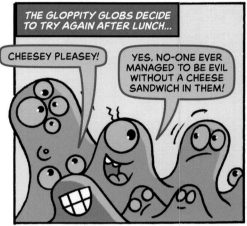

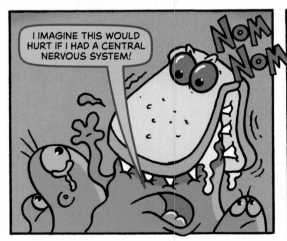

BERYL THE PERIL

SO...

ALL DONE! ISN'T IT A BEAUTY, BERYL?

WHUMP WHUMP

I'M PRETENDING I'M WATCHING YOU ON 'YOOFTUBE'. GOTTA SAY, I DON'T THINK I'LL BE SUBSCRIBING TO YOUR CHANNEL, IT'S PRETTY BORING.

hmph!

MAYBE IT'D BE MORE EXCITING IF YOU WERE *ACTUALLY* HELPING ME!

I'M DEFINITELY *UNLIKING* THIS VID!

boink!

LATER...

WHICH SLEEPING BAG DO YOU WANT, BERYL? THE RED OR THE BLUE?

BERYL?

BERYL? *BERYL!*

RUSTLE!

SHAKE!

CAN'T STOP! I'M WATCHING A *FUNNY ANIMAL VIDEO!* LOOK! IT MUST BE ABOUT TO DO SOMETHING HILARIOUS!

YIKES!

SQUEEEAK!

fwoosh!

Scamper!

GAH! DO SOMETHING FUNNY! COME ON! HOW AM I SUPPOSED TO SHARE IT WITH MY FRIENDS?

COME ON, BERYL. FORGET ABOUT THE INTERNET. WE CAN DO SOMETHING COOL OUT HERE.

LIKE WHAT?

CUDDLES AND DIMPLES

LAYLA VILLE'S EVIL COMPUTER HAS TRAPPED DANDYTOWN IN A GAME...

MY BROTHERS ARE STILL ON THE OUTSIDE! THEY'LL, ER... THEY'LL NOT DO ANYTHING, WILL THEY?

NOPE! I LEFT THEM OUT OF THE GAME SO I CAN TRICK THEM INTO MAKING ME A GIANT ROBOT BODY!

YIKES!

THEY'RE TOO SMART TO BE TRICKED LIKE THAT!

WE WILL SEE!

WHERE DID THE BIG FACE GO?

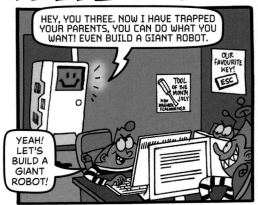

HEY, YOU THREE. NOW I HAVE TRAPPED YOUR PARENTS, YOU CAN DO WHAT YOU WANT! EVEN BUILD A GIANT ROBOT.

OUR FAVOURITE KEY! ESC

TOOL OF THE MONTH JULY NON MAGNETIC SCREWDRIVER

YEAH! LET'S BUILD A GIANT ROBOT!

THEY ARE DOING IT NOW.

ENOUGH TALK. TIME FOR SOME RUNNING AND SCREAMING!

ARRGH!

CORPORAL CLOTT LEAPS INTO ACTION...

NOW TO USE ALL MY YEARS OF SOLDIER TRAINING AND DEFEAT THE BADDIES.

BA-ZOINK!!

WHAT JUST HAPPENED?

I THINK YOU LOST A LIFE.

POP!

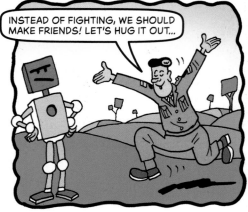

INSTEAD OF FIGHTING, WE SHOULD MAKE FRIENDS! LET'S HUG IT OUT...

BA-ZOINK!!

OR WE COULD RUN!

YOU'VE GOT ONE LIFE LEFT, CLOTT! HOLD ON TO IT!

POP!

Can **YOU** show the Dandy team how it's done by finding a route past the bears to reach the glitch?

FINISH!

START!

SOLUTION

Dinah Mo!
ENVIRONMENTAL INVENTOR!

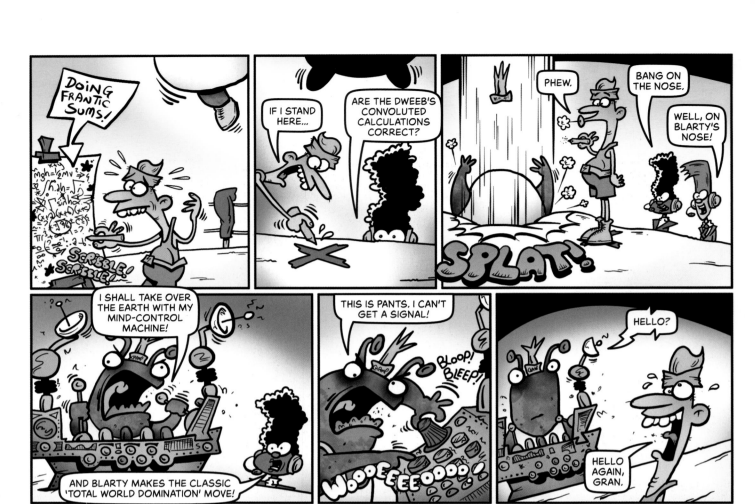

BERYL THE PERIL

WOO-HOO! TIME TO GET OUT THERE AND BRING THE PERIL!

ZOOM!

THE FIRST THING I THINK I'LL DO IS KNOCK THE HATS OFF A POLICE OFFICER OR TWO!

GRR! WHEN WE FIND OUT WHO DID THIS THEY'LL BE IN TROUBLE!

HUH? WHAT GIVES? I HAVEN'T DONE ANYTHING YET!

HMPH! WHATEVER! I'LL DRAW SOME FUNNY PICTURES ON THE TOWN HALL WALLS INSTEAD!

CHALK

SOMEONE'S BEATEN ME TO THAT AS WELL!

DANDYTOWN TOWNHALL

BATTY!

DUH!

YEE HAW!

MEOWCH!

MIN WAS HERE (AND DUCK!)

WAIT! WHAT'S THIS?

MIN WAS HERE (AND DUCK!)

WHO'S MIN? AND WHO'S DUCK?

WHOOSH!

SPLUTCH!

GRR! WHOEVER DID THAT IS IN FOR A WHOLE LOTTA TROUBLE!

I DID THAT. I'M MINNIE, MINNIE THE MINX.

PLEASED TOMATO. CHUCKLE!

HMPH! THAT PUN WAS ROTTEN!

CORPORAL CLOTT

THE ARMY DECIDED THAT THE BEST PLACE FOR CORPORAL CLOTT WAS NOT IN THE ARMY. SO THEY'RE HELPING HIM FIND A DIFFERENT JOB...

IT'S NOT GOING WELL!

CLOTT TRIES TO BE A FIREFIGHTER...

TURN IT OFF! HOW ARE YOU EVEN DOING THAT?! WATER IS MEANT TO COME OUT, *NOT FIRE!*

BUT YOU SAID IT WAS A *FIRE* HOSE!

HE TRIED BEING A LIBRARIAN...

QUIET!!!

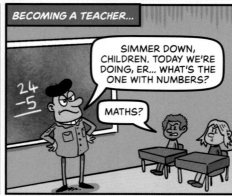

BECOMING A TEACHER...

SIMMER DOWN, CHILDREN. TODAY WE'RE DOING, ER... WHAT'S THE ONE WITH NUMBERS?

MATHS?

SO... 24 MINUS FIVE? TRICKY QUESTION. SO YOU, ER... HOW DO YOU DO THIS AGAIN?

TWENTEEN?!

AND A SIMPLER QUESTION WOULD BE 'FOUR MINUS TWO'. WHICH IS, ERM... I FEEL LIKE I WANT TO SAY THREE?

THEN HE TRIED TO BE A WAITER...

OOPS!

ARRGH!

A MECHANIC...

OOPS!

YOUR PROBLEM IS TOO MUCH TOMATO SOUP IN THE ENGINE.

HOW IS THERE SOUP IN MY ENGINE?

I PUT IT THERE.

WHILE BACK AT THE BASE...

YOU THERE! WASH THE TANKS!

THEY'RE ALREADY WASHED, SIR.

ER... GOOD. AND THEY DIDN'T END UP PINK OR UPSIDE DOWN?

SIR! NO, SIR!

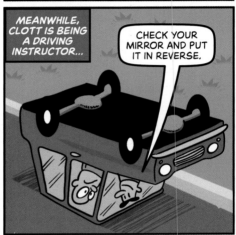

CUDDLES AND DIMPLES

DESPERATE DAN

GOT ME A NEW JOB AS A KEEPER AT CACTUSVILLE ZOO. CAN'T WAIT TO GET STARTED!

SEE TO THE ELEPHANTS FIRST.

COOL!

MANAG OFF

WHERE ARE THE BUNS?

WE DON'T FEED THEM BUNS, BUT THE BUCKET'S NOT FOR FEEDING ANYWAY.

YOU'LL ALSO NEED THIS.

HUH?

GASP! THEM ELEPHANTS HAVE MIGHTY SMELLY POO!

SHUCKS! MISSED ONE.

JUST YOU TRY AND GET IT, BOZO!

EEK!

EXCUSE ME, BUDDY.